Performing Arts Handbook

Grade 2

Printed in the United States of America

ISBN 0-15-309763-9

3 4 5 6 7 8 9 10 073 2000 99

Harcourt Brace & Company

Orlando   Atlanta   Austin   Boston   San Francisco   Chicago   Dallas   New York   Toronto   London

http://www.hbschool.com

Contents

UNIT 1

PERFORMING ARTS PROJECT

ART PRINTS

UNIT 2

PERFORMING ARTS PROJECT

ART PRINTS

UNIT 3

PERFORMING ARTS PROJECT

ART PRINTS

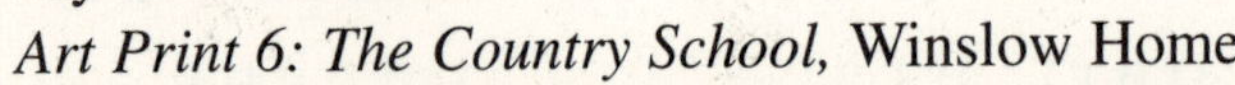
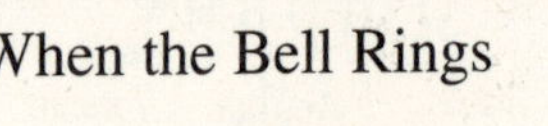

UNIT 4

UNIT 5

UNIT 6

Performing Arts Activities Enrich Visual Arts Instruction

MRS. J.: What is the girl in the painting doing?

MONICA: Watering the flowers.

ALEX: Maybe she is all done with the watering can.

MRS. J.: That could be. Philipé, this week you are watering the plants in our class-room. Could you show us how you do it? *(Philipé demonstrates with a watering can and the plants.)* Great. Do you think you could show us how to do that **without** the watering can? Could you pantomime that for us? *(Philipé pantomimes the action.)* Alex, Josh, and Amy, why don't you join Philipé and pantomime this action for us.

Applying Performing Arts to Visual Arts Instruction

While Mrs. J.'s students have benefited from earlier discussions about *Girl with a Watering Can,* they are beginning to explore creative ways to respond to it using the performing arts. Children are naturally drawn to music, movement, and drama, and many learn best (in any and all content areas) when they can express themselves using the media of music, dance, and/or theater. Additionally, students may approach the kinesthetic and aural performing arts activities with self-confidence that may be lacking when they attempt to create (visual) art.

In the scene on page 4 Mrs. J. shows how to involve her students in the discussion preceeding an activity. She knows that Philipé, who is an ESL student, will be successful with his pantomime. Later on she may have him explain what he did in his pantomime, helping him develop his oral language skills. Alex learns best with kinesthetic activities, so Mrs. J. quickly draws him into the pantomime. Whether Mrs. J. chooses to do the activity with the whole class or small groups, she can use the *Performing Arts Handbook* to develop discussions about art and cultivate students' creative responses.

Using the *Performing Arts Handbook*

The *Performing Arts Handbook* offers two strands of instructional support for ART EXPRESS.

- Unit projects expand on the program unit ideas about the visual arts. A four- to six-week performing arts project culminates in a performance such as a circus, a play, a concert, or a dance. Although the focus of the performing arts project is the performance, students are encouraged to develop their talents and skills (with specific goals for creative expression, artistic perception, historical/cultural context, and aesthetic valuing) during the process. (See pages 6–9 for ideas on how to assess students and manage the classroom during these projects.)
- *Art Print* activities (such as the one Mrs. J. used) provide an opportunity to extend the learning and appreciation of fine art by drawing students into a performing arts response. With these 30–40-minute lessons, students interact with the painting through their imaginations. Suggestions for dance, music, and theater responses are offered for each *Art Print*.

Learning about the visual arts can expand students' interests and creative abilities. Integrating visual and performing arts is a natural way to "grab" student interest. There is no better way to discover students' potential to learn and have fun at the same time!

Also available—

Performing Arts Cassettes:

Grades 1–2 and *Grades 3–5*

•

For each *Art Print* activity,

a music selection from

the *Performing Arts Cassette:*

Grades 1–2 is cited.

Using Project Journals to Manage the Classroom and Assess Students

What is a PROJECT JOURNAL?

Classroom journals can be created and used for all kinds of purposes—to explore concepts learned in math, reading, and science, for example. A project journal is another kind of record that documents the work and the process of a long-term project for a group or an individual student.

If the whole class is collaborating on a single unit project, such as a play or a concert, one journal would be kept for the class. Small groups working on a project would each keep a group journal. A student working independently on a project would keep an individual journal.

Students compile and organize materials in a three-ring binder. The binder becomes a chronological record of all work done by group members.

The journal has several purposes. Students can use it to keep track of their own work on the unit project over the course of several weeks. The teacher benefits from the record of work showing the progress made. The journal is the touchpoint for everyone connected with the project. When group members meet and make decisions, they add to the binder. Students can return to the binder during appropriate work times to check on group and individual work, even if other group members are not present.

What do students write and keep in the binder during the course of the project?

Meeting notes, plans, sketches, lists, research notes, handouts, and records of setbacks are just some of the things students keep in their project journals. Assessment copying masters (such as the ones on pages 58 and 59) may also be filled out and put in the binder. Encourage students to be creative and concerned about keeping the journal up to date.

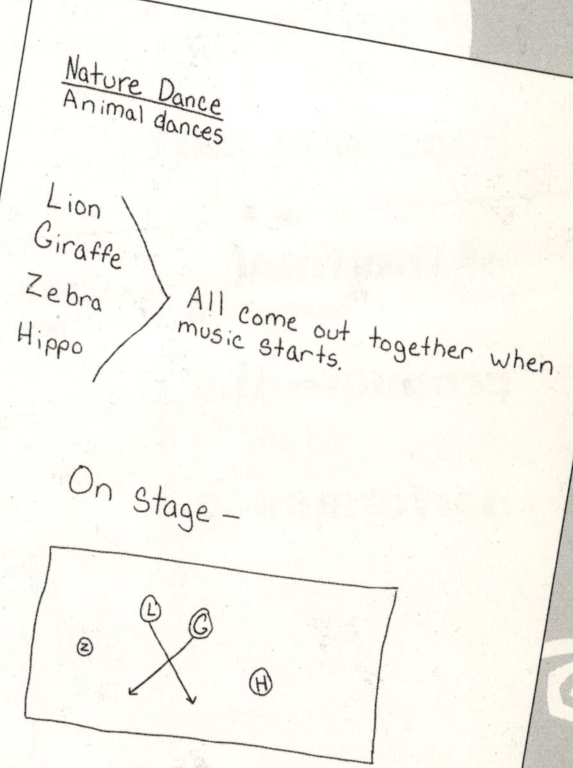

Once students have an understanding of the project goals, they can begin to plan their project using the goals as a guide and the project journal as a means to organize tasks and keep track of progress.

The project journal gives group members

- the opportunity to involve all group members in making decisions that concern the final performance.
- the ability to organize, plan, and record each step of the process, including changes.
- project-related information for peer and self-assessments.

The project journal allows teachers

- to assess students' individual and group efforts, organization, planning, and execution of work as part of the final performance.
- to put decision-making in the hands of students.

The project *process* (recorded in the project journal) is an important part of the final product—the performance.

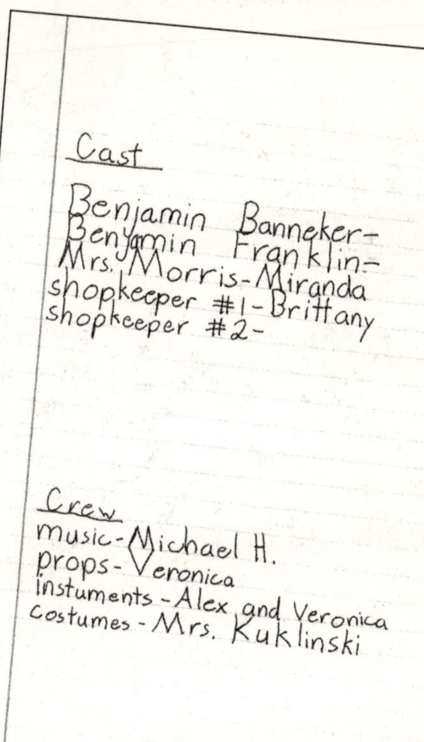

Cast
Benjamin Banneker-
Benjamin Franklin-
Mrs. Morris-Miranda
shopkeeper #1-Brittany
shopkeeper #2-

Crew
music-Michael H.
props-Veronica
instuments-Alex and Veronica
costumes-Mrs. Kuklinski

Tell me more about how the project journal can help students meet individual needs. What about students with special needs?

The opportunity to set project goals and to make choices about how to meet those goals invites students to match the tasks that need to be accomplished with the talents of the group members. Students who prefer not to perform can still take on meaningful tasks. Unit Project lessons guide students as they choose roles and tasks. Recording their responsibilities in the binder makes all group members feel involved and important.

Students with special needs also have special talents. Whether or not they choose to perform, they can participate in group roles that develop and enhance their interaction with group members and build their sense of self-worth. Defining and clarifying group member roles in the project journal—sometimes two or three times during the course of a project—allows all students to identify their part in the group effort.

Who I Want to Be

Unit Project Overview: Children create and enact a short story with dialogue involving interactions of people within a career or occupation.

VOCABULARY CONCEPTS

You may wish to teach these **Glossary** words and concepts in context during the project.

dialogue
character
setting
cast

PROJECT OBJECTIVES

Artistic Perception Observe the environment and respond using movement and voice.

Creative Expression Create and perform structured improvisation; then evaluate it, and perform the piece again.

Historical/Cultural Context View and participate in activities such as storytelling and recounting personal histories. Learn about careers and jobs.

Aesthetic Valuing Discuss the successful use of basic techniques such as dialogue and character portrayal.

① WARM-UP

Choose one of the following activities:

- Have children play a game of charades. Scan the help-wanted ads and develop a list of careers. Write each career on a separate slip of paper. Begin the game with a child drawing a slip of paper and acting out the things that worker does. For example, a chef would be cooking something. When the worker is correctly identified, the person who guessed correctly becomes the next player.

- Tell children they are going to act out events at work. Give partners a scene to act out. Interesting scenes might be between a dentist and a patient, or a police officer and a lost child. Have children explore, through dialogue, problems and resolutions as they think the characters would.

 Have children discuss the following ideas and record responses in their project journals.

- **What kind of worker would you like to be?**
- **What can you do to make your character come alive?**

❷ PLAN THE PROJECT

Set Goals Explain to children that, with a partner or group, they will act out a story about people in their jobs. Help children with the following project goals:

- create, remember, and enact a short story with dialogue
- perform with one or more children in a class presentation
- produce a meaningful, cohesive performance

Outline the Project Plan with children how to do the project. Consider:

- the scope of the project (see Project Options)
- the intended audience—the class, parents, another class
- careers the class would like to focus on so partners or small groups can decide which occupations to portray
- research needed: what specific workers do, what they wear, how they do their jobs, who they interact with, and problems they might have

Before children begin, make a large jobs chart, listing all the different people who work in a career field such as medicine, education, retail sales, community service, arts, entertainment, and sports. If the project requires them, now is the time to choose a Wardrobe Supervisor, Stage Manager, Set Designer, and any other people necessary for the production.

Once partners or groups have been organized, children should begin identifying and defining tasks. All partner and group work can be recorded in separate sections of the project journal.

❸ EXPLORE THEATER IDEAS

- Children should chose individual roles for their stories. They can use the Character Profile on the copying master on page 13 to help them.

- Have children experiment with possible dialogue and action that might take place between the characters.

- Suggest that children switch roles and critique each other's role-playing.

SCHOOL-HOME CONNECTION

Have a Career Day. Invite one or more workers to visit the class and talk about their careers. They can discuss their specific work, educational requirements, special clothing, problems they may have, and other facets of their occupations.

CLASSROOM MANAGEMENT
Before dress rehearsals, have each group make checklists of day-of-the-performance tasks and assignments.

 **For Students with Special Needs**
Role-playing may be difficult for some special-needs children, so pair a helpful child with the special-needs student.

CAREERS IN ART

Children should be aware of these theater-related careers as they work on this project.
- **wardrobe supervisor**
- **theater arts teacher**
- **playwright**
- **set/prop designer**
- **stage manager**
- **camera operator**

❹ CREATE DIALOGUES

- As children create their dialogues, they may continue using the copying master on page 13.
- The Prop Manager should gather any props needed.
- Costumes and sets should now be planned and started.

❺ REHEARSE AND REFINE

- Have all groups or partners rehearse their performances.
- Have at least one dress rehearsal to run through the entire performance from beginning to end.
- Children who are not performing should help coordinate the set, costume, and prop needs of others. They can also make programs and arrange chairs for the audience.

❻ PERFORM IT!

Some options for the performance include:
- videotaping the performance so it can be shown in the media center to other classes
- writing and publishing the dialogues on the school's World Wide Web site

Performance and Process Assessments
Review with children the project journals and their performances based on the goals set at the beginning of the project. Encourage children to add personal evaluations and responses to the project journals.

✔ **For the Student**
- How did you like playing a "character"?
- Which part of this project did you most enjoy?

✔ **For the Teacher**
- Did all the partners or groups cooperate with each other?
- How well did children use dialogue to portray their characters?

Name _______________________________

PERFORMING ARTS PROJECT

Who I Want to Be

Developing a Character Profile

Use this sheet as you decide who your character will be. Write all the things about your character. Then list problems your character may have, how your character will solve the problem, and what your character's dialogue will be.

Name of character _______________________________

Character's job _______________________________

Character's costume (work clothes) _______________________________

Character's props (special tools) _______________________________

Setting (where the character works) _______________________________

Cast (people who work with the character) _______________________________

____

Problems the character may have _______________________________

How the character will solve the problems _______________________________

____

Dialogue (what the character says) _______________________________

____

Sounds for Everyone

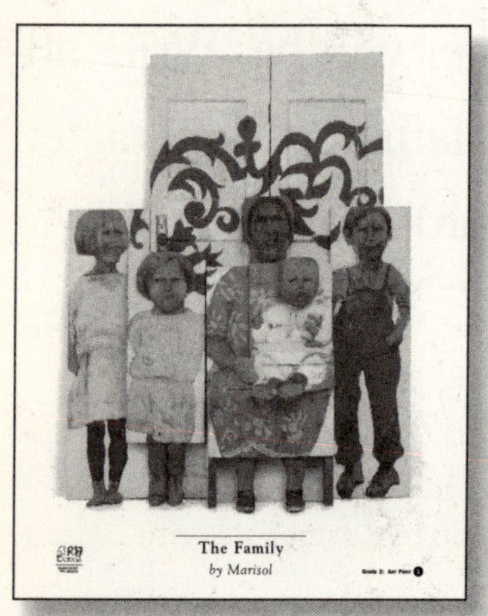

▲ **Art Print 1,** *The Family,*
Marisol

OBJECTIVE: Children identify simple forms and elements of music and choose sounds to describe family members.

MATERIALS: *Art Print 1, Performing Arts Cassette:* "Not Far from Here," "Peter and the Wolf," Live Oak Media, (ISBN 0-87499-074-20), six or more water glasses, rod for tapping, paper, tape

TIPS AND TIME-SAVERS Borrow several tape recorders from other teachers or the media center to speed up the groups' music selections.

ⓔ WARM-UP

Play "Not Far from Here" as children look at *Art Print 1, The Family.* Then discuss the following questions:

- **What are some things that you notice in this picture?**

- **If the members of this family all stood and lined up from tallest to shortest, what would that order be?**

- **Look at the heads of the people. Which ones are high? Which are lower? How did the artist make some heads an even height?**

ⓔ MUSIC ACTIVITY

To help children distinguish high and low sounds, use this simple technique. Place several water glasses in small paper bags so children cannot see in or through them. Put different amounts of water in the glasses, and set them in no particular order. Have children tap the sides of the glasses and discover which sounds are high and which are low in pitch.

Then have children arrange the glasses in sequence, either from low to high or high to low, and tap the glasses in sequence.

Ask children to think about the sounds they have made and *Art Print 1, The Family*. Ask them to choose one of the sounds for each family member. Then ask:

- **Why did you choose that sound for the mother?**

- **Which sound did you choose for the baby? The boy? The girls? Why?**

Continue by having groups of children listen to several recorded musical selections. Just as they selected a single sound for each family member, have them select a piece of music for each member. Allow time for listening to many pieces.

 REFLECT

Gather children in front of *The Family*. Discuss which piece of music was selected for each family member by the groups, and play them one at a time for the class. Have the class tell whether they think the musical selections were good choices. Play "Not Far from Here," and have children tell whether they think the music is appropriate for *The Family*. Then discuss the following questions:

- **What can you say about how the members of this family feel?**

- **What would you like to say to the artist?**

Informal Assessment

✔ Were children able to distinguish high and low sounds, and were they able to place them in order?

✔ Were children able to evaluate the work of others?

THE SOUNDS OF MUSIC

Have children perform a simple dramatization of a musical work such as "Peter and the Wolf." Have children evaluate how the music helped their interpretation of the characters. ■ GOAL: CREATIVE EXPRESSION

FAMILY CIRCLE DANCES

Have groups of children form circles and experiment with dancing by circling to the right during a certain part of some music and circling to the left during the other part. Have children add variations to their dances by clapping, stamping, hopping, moving high and low, raising and lowering arms, or performing other movements. ■ GOAL: CREATIVE EXPRESSION

From Seed to Flower

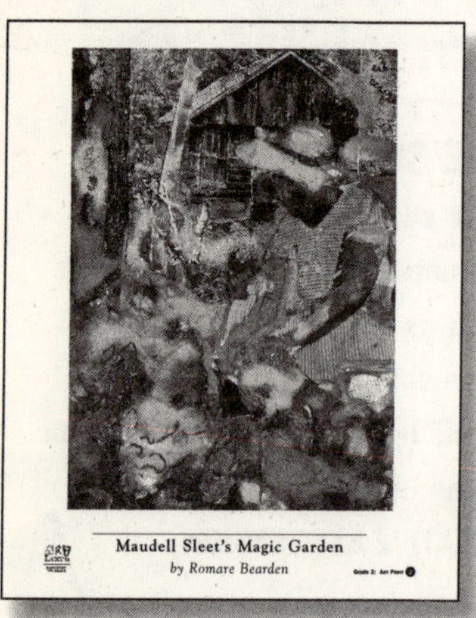

Maudell Sleet's Magic Garden
by Romare Bearden

▲ **Art Print 2,** *Maudell Sleet's Magic Garden,* Romare Bearden

OBJECTIVE: Children create an interpretive improvised dance sequence showing life from a plant's point of view.

MATERIALS: *Art Print 2, Performing Arts Cassette:* "Garden Song" and "Dancin' in Rhythm"

CLASSROOM MANAGEMENT Try experimenting with the movement activities at the same time as children are experimenting. Your movements may provide a model for children less willing to experiment on their own. As an additional benefit, you may find the activity very relaxing.

WARM-UP

Create a "jazz" mood by playing Dave Brubeck's "Dancin' in Rhythm." Tell children this form of music is called jazz. Explain that Romare Bearden thinks of his paintings as music and is greatly influenced by jazz. Display *Maudell Sleet's Magic Garden,* and ask volunteers to tell what they see.

- **Does this picture remind you of a place you've been to? Tell about it.**

- **How do you think the person doing the gardening feels?**

- **Why do you think the artist used such bright colors?**

DANCE ACTIVITY

Begin by taking the class into an open space. Ask children to move one hand in as many different ways as they can. Next, have children experiment with moving their arms, wrists, elbows, shoulders, and heads. Have children sit on the floor and experiment with leg and foot movements. Continue by having children lie on the floor. Tell them to think about some of the moves they experimented with as you guide them through the following improvisation:

- **Imagine that you are in a garden like the one you saw. You are a tiny flower seed, and someone has put you under the ground. Show with your body what you are like as a little round seed under the ground.**

- **Now the sun has come out, and you are beginning to sprout. How do you feel? How can you show this with body moves? Are you ready to stand up yet?**

- **You are growing out of the ground and becoming a plant. Are you stretching or bending? How do you feel?**

- **Finally, you are a flower. Your blossom is in full bloom. What do you feel like now? Show how you would move your body like a proud new plant.**

Remind children to think about the flowers they saw in *Maudell Sleet's Magic Garden.* Allow time for performances by groups of three or four. Children can also demonstrate the life of a flower accompanied only by music, without the guiding narration. Consider having some groups perform for another class.

◉ REFLECT

Have children view *Maudell Sleet's Magic Garden* again. Play "Garden Song" in the background as children study the painting. Then discuss the following questions:

- **Now that you have experienced how a flower moves and feels as it grows from a seed, is there anything you see in the painting that you didn't see before?**

- **The style of this artwork is called collage. A collage is a collection of many different materials, shapes, and colors. Why do you think the artist chose this technique to show Maudell Sleet's garden?**

- **Why do you think he called it a *magic* garden?**

Informal Assessment

✔ Did children fully explore the movement activities, and were they able to adapt the movement to a rhythm?

✔ How did children view *Maudell Sleet's Magic Garden* in a more imaginative way after their movement experiences?

YOU DON'T SAY? Ask pairs of children to create dialogues between two seeds that are planted and grow into plants. Encourage children to give the plants some problems, such as a windstorm or too much water. Have them write and share their dialogues with the class. ■ GOAL: CREATIVE EXPRESSION

SING MY SONG Have children make up a song to tell about the life of a plant. Suggest that they think of familiar tunes and then create new lyrics. For example, the tune for "Frère Jacques" can be used to become "I'm a little seed, I'm a little seed, Under the ground, Under the ground. . . ." Have children perform their songs. ■ GOAL: CREATIVE EXPRESSION

Rhythm Band

Unit Project Overview: Children use a variety of common items to make rhythm band instruments. They use the instruments to learn about and perform rhythms.

MATERIALS

- wooden blocks (hand size), round oatmeal boxes, small dowel rods, cans with lids, paper plates, dry beans, empty coconut shells, wooden spoons, shoe boxes
- filmstrip: *Music Adventures of Lollipop Dragon®* series, "The Lollipop Dragon Rhythm Band" (SVE, 1995)

VOCABULARY CONCEPTS

You may wish to teach these **Glossary** words and concepts in context during the project.

tempo
rhythm
band
beat

CROSS-CURRICULAR CONNECTIONS

Fine Arts Music, Art
Science Sound
Language Arts Reading/ Syllables, Writing, Speaking, Listening
Social Studies Cooperation
Math Counting

PROJECT OBJECTIVES

Artistic Perception Use a simple system to note and read rhythms.

Creative Expression Use common items to create rhythm instruments. Improvise simple rhythmic patterns. Perform in rhythm and maintain a steady beat.

Historical/Cultural Context Identify various instruments and learn about their origins.

Aesthetic Valuing Evaluate performances by others using the terms *rhythm, tempo, beat,* and *rhythm pattern.*

① WARM-UP

Choose one of the following activities:

- Begin rhythm exploration by having children clap the syllables in their names. Then have them experiment with names of cars, pies, insects, or whatever seems like fun and can yield an awareness of the rhythm of syllables. Then try some of the names again, and ask children to write a mark for each syllable they say or hear.

- Have children sing some familiar songs while clapping out the words. Some good songs for clapping are *Bingo, A-Hunting We Will Go,* and *Here We Go 'Round the Mulberry Bush.* Organize the class into two groups. Have one group clap the syllables of the song while the other group claps a steady beat. Show children how to count out a 4/4 beat.

Have children discuss the following ideas and record responses in their project journals.

- **What is rhythm? Name as many places as you can where we can find rhythm.** (ocean waves, heartbeat)
- **In what ways, other than clapping, could you make rhythms?**

❷ PLAN THE PROJECT

Set Goals Explain to children that they will create instruments and perform rhythms together in a rhythm band. Help children with the following project goals:

- make instruments; then create, remember, and perform a rhythm pattern
- perform with a group, synchronizing play with others
- produce a meaningful, cohesive performance

Outline the Project Plan with children how to do the project. Consider:

- the scope of the project (see Project Options)
- the audience—such as community members or younger children
- which instrument children would like to make
- research needed: people's first instruments; kinds of sounds produced by striking, blowing, or strumming instruments

Once small groups have been organized, children should begin identifying and defining tasks for their group. All group work can be recorded in separate sections of the project journal.

❸ EXPLORE AND MAKE RHYTHM INSTRUMENTS

- Children should choose individual roles for the project, such as a Conductor for each band or a Production Director.

- Children choose materials for their rhythm instruments. They may want to experiment with various materials before making their final decisions.

- Children make their rhythm instruments.

PROJECT OPTIONS

- Rather than make instruments, have children use two pencils as rhythm sticks or use hand clapping to create rhythm patterns. **SIMPLE**

- Have groups make rhythm instruments from common objects, then create and perform rhythm patterns. Children will perform for others as a Rhythm Band, complete with costumes. **ELABORATE**

Invite parents to be a part of the production by asking them to furnish the materials needed for the instruments or to help with costumes.

CLASSROOM MANAGEMENT

If children are not yet able to note rhythms or have difficulty doing so, you may omit the notation and use the copying master as an individual planner for children's activities in their groups.

For Students with Special Needs

Hearing-impaired children can participate in these activities with visual cues from another child. With these cues they will know when to play their rhythms.

CAREERS IN ART

Children should be aware of these music-related careers as they work on this project.

director (band, choral, music)

percussionist

instrumentalist

composer

❹ CREATE RHYTHM PATTERNS

- Have children use their instruments to experiment with different tempos as well as different rhythms. They may need music to accompany them at first, but later they should be able to perform by using rhythms alone.
- Children should experiment with playing different rhythm patterns at the same time, as another player keeps a steady beat.
- As children begin to put their rhythm ideas together, encourage them to think of a beginning, a middle, and an ending for their total compositions.
- Using the copying master on page 21 as a guide for noting the rhythms, have children record their rhythms so they can remember them and teach them to others.
- If desired, costumes should now be made.

❺ REHEARSE AND REFINE

- Children rehearse the performance, with all the bands performing in the order of the final production.
- Have at least one full rehearsal to run through the performance from beginning to end.

❻ PERFORM IT!

Some options for the performance include:
- videotaping the performance so it may be shown at a local senior center or shared with other community members
- setting up a stage in an outdoor setting

Performance and Process Assessments

Review with children the project journals and their performances based on the goals set at the beginning of the project. Encourage children to add personal evaluations and responses to the project journals.

✔ **For the Student**
- Which rhythms and instrument do you like best?
- Did you play your rhythms the way you had planned?

✔ **For the Teacher**
- Were children able to plan their performances?
- How creative were children in devising instruments and rhythms? Did they value their own work?

Name _______________________________

Rhythm Band

Writing Rhythm Patterns

Use this sheet as you decide which **rhythm** each person in the band will play. Write a mark for each **beat**, using the system shown. When you have written the rhythms, play them and decide what **tempo**, or speed, you will use as you play.

|	=	1 beat
⊓	=	2 beats
⊓⊓	=	4 beats
⊓⊓⊓⊓	=	8 beats

First band member plays:

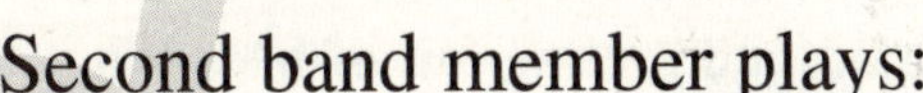

____

Second band member plays:

____

Third band member plays:

____

Fourth band member plays:

____

Working the Land

Harvest at La Crau
by Vincent van Gogh

▲ **Art Print 3,** *Harvest at La Crau,* Vincent van Gogh

OBJECTIVE: Each child pantomimes activities done on a farm.

MATERIALS: *Art Print 3, Performing Arts Cassette:* "The merry peasant returning from work (The Happy Farmer)"

CLASSROOM MANAGEMENT Give visual learners a chance to view the actions of others before they participate with their own pantomimes. Using a partner may also be helpful.

◎ WARM-UP

Begin by asking children to tell what they know about farm chores, and list their responses. A list might include feeding animals, plowing the fields, and harvesting crops. Then display *Harvest at La Crau,* and ask volunteers to describe what they see. Add to the list farm chores that are being done in the scene.

- **What is the season of the year in the painting?**

- **What are the people in the painting doing?**

- **Why do you think the artist chose this scene to paint?**

◎ THEATER ACTIVITY

Have children stand in a large circle. Tell them they are going to pantomime a day in the life of a farmer and do farm chores from the picture, including some from the list.

- **Imagine that you are the farmer in the painting. You are just waking up and getting out of bed. What do you hear that tells you it's time to get up and start your day?**

- **Now you're getting your breakfast. What are you eating? What are some of the smells in the kitchen?**

- **You are going out to start your chores, beginning with the animals. Which animals will you tend to first? What will you do for them?**

- **After the animals are taken care of, you have to tend to the crops. Today is the day you will cut the wheat and put hay up into the haystacks. How will you do that?**

To continue the farmer's day, tell children that they may work in pairs or small groups. Each group can brainstorm what will happen next in the farmer's day and then pantomime it. Allow time for each group to perform for the class. Have children refer to *Art Print 3* to get ideas for the rest of the farmer's day.

◎ REFLECT

Gather children in front of *Harvest at La Crau*. Play "The merry peasant returning from work (The Happy Farmer)" from the *Performing Arts Cassette* as children study the painting. Then discuss the following:

- **Now that you've acted out a day in the life of a farmer, what do you see in the painting that you didn't see before?**

- **What would you see in the painting if it showed a different season of the year?**

- **What message do you think van Gogh was trying to give about farms and working on farms in this painting?**

Informal Assessment

✔ Which movements did children use to communicate effectively with pantomime? Which children learned from watching others?

✔ What new insights into the painting do children now have?

WORKING SONGS Play the song "Oklahoma!" from the Rodgers and Hammerstein musical *Oklahoma!* or use another up-tempo song. Have children try pantomiming to the fast tempo of the music. Ask children to reflect on farmwork of the past and farmwork of today. ■ GOAL: HISTORICAL/CULTURAL CONTEXT

WORKING DANCES Have children perform their pantomimes as rhythmic movements. Put several of their movements together with a music background to form a "Working the Land" dance. ■ GOAL: CREATIVE EXPRESSION

Move Like a Cat

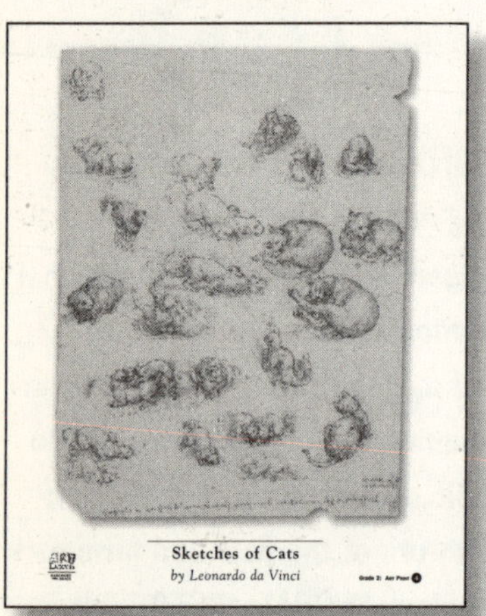

▲ Art Print 4, *Sketches of Cats,*
Leonardo da Vinci

OBJECTIVE: Children create a series of catlike movements and put them together to form an interpretive dance.

MATERIALS: *Art Print 4, Performing Arts Cassette:* "Duetto buffo di due gatti (Cats' Duet)"

TIPS AND TIME-SAVERS Children may be helped to remember movements they create by having one child demonstrate a movement and then having another child do that movement and add another movement to the first move.

◎ WARM-UP

Show *Sketches of Cats*. Have children study and comment on the various poses the artist used as he sketched the cats. Ask children to list all the ways that cats appear to be moving in the artwork. Record their responses in a list. Responses may include jumping, lying, walking, leaping, stretching, turning, rolling, tumbling, crouching, and pouncing.

- **What do you think Leonardo da Vinci was trying to show as he made these sketches of cats?**

- **Do you see any animals other than cats in the sketches?**

◎ DANCE ACTIVITY

Clear a large area, and make sure each child has space in which to move and lie down. If space is limited, work with small groups. Tell children they are going to try to move like cats. As they move, ask them to recall *Sketches of Cats* and the list of movements they made. Guide their movements with the following:

- **Imagine you are a cat. Show how you would jump and roll.**

- **Imagine you are a cat rolling a ball of yarn across the floor. Now someone is holding the yarn above your head.**

- **Show how you would move as a cat trying to coax a mouse out of its hole and then trying to catch the mouse.**

- **Imagine someone is brushing your fur.**

- **Now try some cat moves of your own.**

Have children choose partners to try the movements together. For example, partners could bat the ball of yarn to one another. Put on some music, and let the music guide the movement. Children may do a few of the moves together and make up a short dance with them. Later, have the partners take turns performing for the rest of the class. Following each performance, have others tell what they saw and liked about the performers' dances. Ask them to tell what kinds of movements they saw that reminded them of the cats in *Art Print 4*.

◎ REFLECT

Take time after the dances to have children once again view *Sketches of Cats*. Play "Duetto buffo di due gatti (Cats' Duet)" as they study the sketches. Then discuss the following:

- **How did the artist's sketches help you know how cats move?**

- **What can you tell family members about this art?**

Informal Assessment

✔ Which children were willing to take risks in their performances? How did they do it?

✔ How were children's performances imaginative and creative?

ACT IT OUT Discuss the musical *Cats* with children, or let them tell about cats they've seen in books or in movies. Have children act out a cat story. Stories to act out may include the poem "The Three Little Kittens," part of the movie *Lion King,* or the book *Nine-in-One Grr! Grr!* by Blia Xiong, adapted by Cathy Spagnoli. Children's Book Press, 1993.
■ **GOAL: HISTORICAL/CULTURAL CONTEXT**

COPYCAT SINGERS Ask children to sing the words "I'm a copycat." They may sing the words using any note or combination of notes. Then have other children listen to what has been sung and sing back the notes they heard.
■ **GOAL: CREATIVE EXPRESSION**

Space Explorers Dance

Unit Project Overview: As children discover the relation-ships between art and peoples' stories, they create a dance using the exploration of space as a theme.

MATERIALS

- *Performing Arts Cassette:* "Golliwog's Cake-Walk," other recorded music
- rhythm band instruments
- videotape: *The Nutcracker* (National Video Corporation, 1985)

VOCABULARY CONCEPTS

You may wish to teach these **Glossary** words and concepts in context during the project.

audience
ballet
dance
locomotor movement
notation

CROSS-CURRICULAR CONNECTIONS

Fine Arts Dance, Music
Science Space, Machines Weightlessness
Social Studies Careers
Math Counting
Language Arts Reading, Writing, Listening, Speaking

PROJECT OBJECTIVES

Artistic Perception Demonstrate spatial concepts through movement at different levels.

Creative Expression Improvise dances based on auditory stimuli; perform dance sequences for classmates describing how different tempos make them feel.

Historical/Cultural Context Watch a videotape of a historical dance form and describe what children see and feel.

Aesthetic Valuing Discuss the differences among the dances developed by the groups, with an emphasis on how dance elements of *time, space,* and *force* were used by each group.

① WARM-UP

Choose one of the following activities:

- Move children to an open place with plenty of room for loco-motor movement exploration. Ask them to think of how it might feel to be weightless in space. Have children explore the smooth, slow-motion action involved in walking, bending, or stretching in space. Have children try the moves again with music. Ask them to move up high and then down low. Show *The Nutcracker* videotape or another ballet, and have children compare weightlessness to ballet moves.

- Have children mimic some robot-like movements. Encourage volunteers to demonstrate their movements for the rest of the class. Play some machine-like music such as "Golliwog's Cake-Walk" while children experiment.

 Have children discuss the following ideas and record their responses in their project journals.

- **What did you do to show astronaut or robot moves?**
- **How did adding music help you with your movements?**

❷ PLAN THE PROJECT

Set Goals Explain to children that they will create and perform a Space Dance. Help children with the following project goals:
  - create, remember, and perform a space dance (possibilities include Weightless Walk, Shuttle Shuffle, and Robot Dance)
  - dance with a group, synchronizing movements with others
  - produce a cohesive, meaningful performance

Outline the Project Plan with children how to do the project. Consider:
  - the scope of the project (see Project Options)
  - the size of the dance group; one large dance group or several small groups performing different dances
  - the audience—such as families or younger children
  - the research needed, such as viewing filmstrips and videotapes to learn more about people in space

Once decisions have been made, children should begin identifying tasks for their group. All group work can be recorded in separate sections of the project journal.

❸ EXPLORE DANCE IDEAS

- Children should choose individual roles for the project, such as Director, Dance Captain(s), and Set and Prop Managers.

- The group or groups decide which dance they want to do.

- Children can choose music for their dances. They may want to play rhythm instruments. The same rhythm band can perform for all the dance groups, or other recorded music may be used.

- Have children experiment with different tempos as they move in slow or fast motion and in high, medium, or low space.

Have a parent contact NASA directly though the World Wide Web or by letter to request free information to share with the class.

CLASSROOM MANAGEMENT

Let children be responsible for creating an area where dancers can move safely. Have them move the furniture away and put it back when the activity or performance is over. Help them plan for safety in both dancing and furniture moving.

 **For Students with Special Needs**

Have children with limited motor skills take an active role in the dances. Have groups plan adaptations of their dances with those students in mind.

CAREERS IN ART

Children should be aware of these dance-related careers as they work on this project.

choreographer
dancer
dance instructor
director

❹ CREATE A DANCE

- As children create their dances, have them write notation about what they are doing. For example, they can make a list of the movements in the dance: step, reach, half turn, step, reach.
- Costume making should be in progress. Children can use newspapers, cardboard boxes, trash bags, aluminum foil, or other materials of their choice for costumes.

❺ REHEARSE AND REFINE

- Children should rehearse the complete performance.
- Children should have at least one dress rehearsal to run through the performance from beginning to end, with dancers in costume.
- Children who are not performing may help coordinate the group's dances and audio needs, or write programs and invitations for the performance.

❻ PERFORM IT!

Some options for the performance include:
- videotaping the performance so it can be shown to other classes or shared with family members who are not able to attend
- having one or two dance groups perform each day as part of a space unit of study

Performance and Process Assessments

Review with children the project journals and their performances based on the goals set at the beginning of the project. Encourage children to add personal evaluations and responses to the project journals.

✔ **For the Student**
- Which do you think was your best dance? Why?
- How did the audience react to your performance?

✔ **For the Teacher**
- How effective were students in conveying a dance about people in space?
- How were plans and group interactions indicative of the final performance?

Name ____

Space Explorers Dance

Learning How to View a Dance

Watching a dance can be more fun when you can talk about what you thought was exciting and how the dancers' movements let you know what the dance was about. Also, you can tell what could have been done better, and what the dancers did that you really liked. All these things can help you enjoy the dance more. Use this sheet when you view a dance.

Names of people in the group _______________________________

____

Name of the dance _______________________________________

Kind of dance ____

What was exciting? _______________________________________

Which movements showed what the dance was about? _________

____

What would have made the dance better? ___________________

____

I really liked ____

____

My Kind of Music

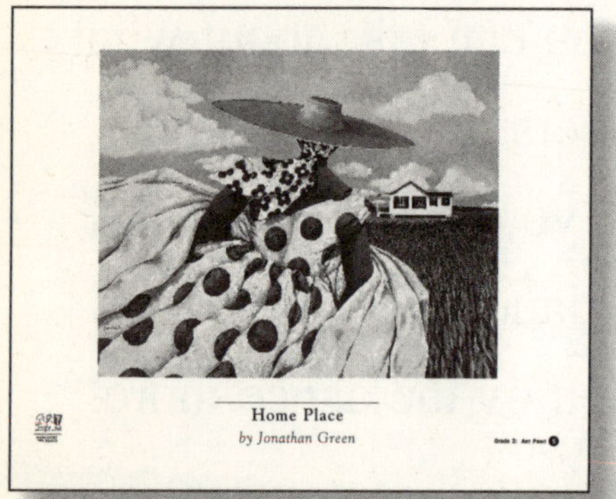

Home Place
by Jonathan Green

▲ **Art Print 5,** *Home Place,*
Jonathan Green

OBJECTIVE: Children select music they'd like to listen to and vote for class favorites.

MATERIALS: *Art Print 5, Performing Arts Cassette:* "Come on Home"

TIPS AND TIME-SAVERS You may want to try the dance activities as transitions. For example, walking on eggs may be done as children are lining up to go to the cafeteria.

⊚ WARM-UP

Display *Art Print 5,* and allow children to discuss the artist's style and the painting's title. Ask children to speculate about why the artist chose to paint the woman from the back and why he chose the colors he did. Then discuss the following questions:

- **How does the woman in the painting appear to be moving?**

- **What words would you use to describe the scene? The woman's clothes?**

- **What kind of music does this painting make you think of?**

⊚ MUSIC ACTIVITY

Discuss that the artist made many choices as he painted *Home Place*. Discuss choices children can make—for example, the games they play or music they listen to. Play any selection from the cassette. Ask children to tell what they like about the piece. Encourage them to identify the instruments and to use terms such as *tempo, rhythm,* and *mood* when they talk about the music. Continue playing selections from the cassette. Then play "Come on Home," and discuss the following questions:

- **What kind of rhythm does the music have?**

- **What pictures form in your mind as you listen to this song?**

- **What does this music make you feel like doing?**

- **Would you like to hear a lot of music like this?**

Prepare sign-up sheets to go along with each of the selections on the cassette, and have children listen to them once again. Have children vote for their favorite song(s) by writing their names on the appropriate sheets. After everyone has listened and signed the sheets, have children count the number of signatures for each selection and discuss class preferences.

◎ REFLECT

Play "Come on Home" as children study *Home Place* again. Then have a few volunteers play their "at home" music as the class looks at the painting. Discuss the following questions:

- **Why do you think the artist painted the woman from the back?**

- **What do you think the woman in the painting looks like? Draw a picture of the woman's face.**

- **How is your picture like the one Jonathan Green painted?**

Informal Assessment

✔ Were children able to tell what they like or dislike about the painting?

✔ Were children able to relate the music to the painting?

GOING HOME Have children pantomime the different ways they could move as they walk home. For example, they could walk as though they are walking on hot pavement, walking on slime, or walking on eggs.
■ **GOAL: CREATIVE EXPRESSION**

WHO IS SHE? Have children think about the character in the painting. Then have them make a list of words to describe the character. Ask children to keep those words in mind as they portray the woman. Have children explore how the woman would walk, talk, and move. ■ **GOAL: CREATIVE EXPRESSION**

When the Bell Rings

The Country School
by Winslow Homer

▲ **Art Print 6,** *The Country School,* Winslow Homer

OBJECTIVE: Children plan and perform improvisations, using simple props in a variety of scenes.

MATERIALS: *Art Print 6, Performing Arts Cassette:* Mozart's "Variations on 'Ah vous dirai-je, maman,'" bell, paper fan, pail, cleaning cloth, small glass

CLASSROOM MANAGEMENT As children set up the performing stations, have them think of things they might use as substitute props if the "real thing" is not available. They may also want to make some of the props.

◎ WARM-UP

Display *The Country School* and have children describe what they see. Arrange an area of the classroom to look like the setting of the painting. Ask a few children to position themselves in the same places as the children and teacher in the painting. Discuss any of the following:

- **What are the children in the painting doing? What is the teacher doing? Does the painting show school activities that are the same as those we do, or are they different?**

- **What things are the same in the painting and in our classroom? What things are different?**

◎ THEATER ACTIVITY

Ask children to imagine what it might have been like to go to a school like the one in the painting. Ask them to name some things children had to do in the old days. For example, children had to collect and bring in firewood for the stove, pump water from a well, ring the school bell, fan themselves when they were hot, sweep floors, write with pens and ink, clean the inkwells (explain that an inkwell is a built-in ink bottle in a desk), and wash the chalkboards. Help children set up and label one "performing station" for one activity, complete with a few simple props. Have a few children take turns dramatizing the activity at the station. Use a bell as a signal to start and stop the activity.

- **When the bell rings, begin showing how you would do the activity from the school days of long ago. What can you do to let people know how you feel about what you are doing?**

- **What did you think about as you did the activity? Is this something you would enjoy doing for a long time or a short time?**

Continue by having children set up several performing stations. Then have a child in each station dramatize the activity. When the bell rings, have children move to the next station. Continue in this manner until everyone has rotated through all the stations. Remind children to keep in mind the children in *Art Print 6* as they are dramatizing.

◉ REFLECT

Group children together in front of *The Country School*. Play "Variations on 'Ah vous dirai-je, maman'" to set the mood and tone for discussion of the painting. Then discuss the following:

- **Now that you've acted out some of the things from the past, what did you learn about school life for the children in the painting?**

- **How would this painting be different if Winslow Homer had decided to paint a city school?**

- **Why do you think the artist painted this scene?**

Informal Assessment

✔ Were children able to communicate ideas about the painting effectively by using improvisation?

✔ Were children able to use props to enhance the activity?

COPYCAT Have children work with a partner. One partner should demonstrate a series of improvised actions for the other to copy. Have them begin by doing one action at a time and then two actions. Keep adding actions. Some sample actions might be climbing a rope, having a tug-of war, jumping rope, or playing hopscotch. ■ **GOAL: CREATIVE EXPRESSION**

WHISTLE WHILE YOU WORK Have children listen to several selections on the *Performing Arts Cassette* and decide which one would be the best one to listen to while they work. Discuss different kinds of work and music best suited for various activities. For example, a lively song could help cleaning go faster. ■ **GOAL: AESTHETIC VALUING**

Folk Songs Tell a Story

Unit Project Overview: Children learn about the oral tradition of folk songs in America. Children learn and sing songs, and then perform them in a history/heritage production.

MATERIALS

- rhythm band instruments
- videotape: *Our Heritage of American Patriotic Songs* (SVE, 1995)*
- * also available in filmstrips with sound recordings

VOCABULARY CONCEPTS

You may wish to teach these **Glossary** words and concepts in context during the project.

> **folk music**
> **elements of music**
> **staff**

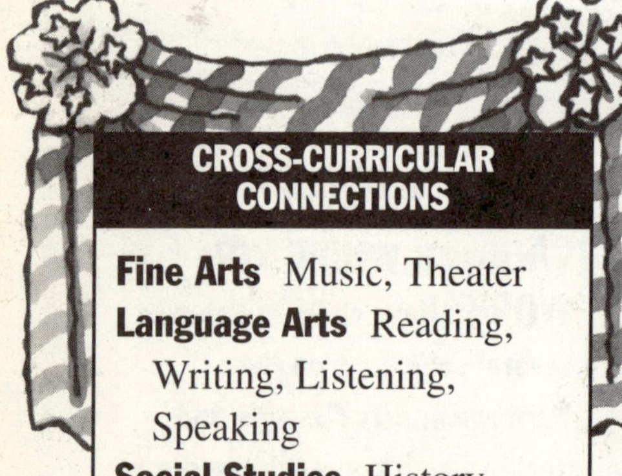

CROSS-CURRICULAR CONNECTIONS

Fine Arts Music, Theater
Language Arts Reading, Writing, Listening, Speaking
Social Studies History
Math Counting, Measuring

PROJECT OBJECTIVES

Artistic Perception Listen to and analyze folk song lyrics.

Creative Expression Group songs according to a theme and sing them in a performance.

Historical/Cultural Context Develop an understanding of the relationship of music to history and culture.

Aesthetic Valuing Make judgments about the quality of musical experiences and performances.

❶ WARM-UP

Choose one of the following activities:

- Have children use songbooks to sing a number of folk songs. Discuss how people sing songs when something is happening in their lives or in their country. Point out how *Sweet Betsy from Pike* is really about pioneers going west. Have children find and discuss similar songs.

- Have a sing-along of patriotic songs with the videotape *Our Heritage of American Patriotic Songs*. Explain what patriotic songs are, and help children learn a few of them. Help children identify the historical era of these songs.

Have children discuss the following ideas and record responses in their project journals.

- **Which songs do I like to sing best?**
- **How are songs used to tell America's story?**

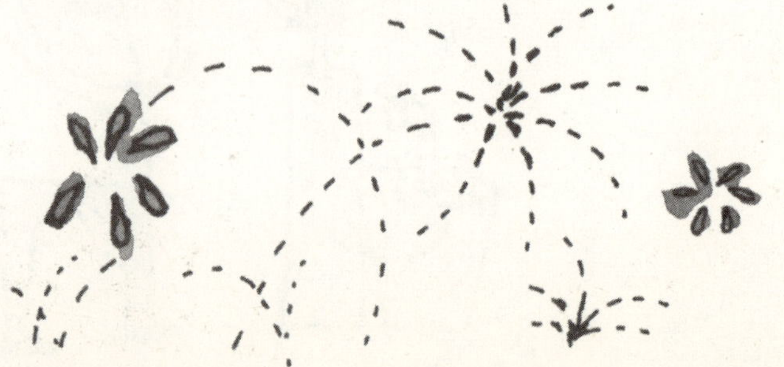

❷ PLAN THE PROJECT

Set Goals Explain to children that they will form groups and sing songs to tell about a time in the history of America. Help children with the following project goals:

- create, remember, and perform songs
- produce a cohesive, meaningful performance with a group keeping together while singing

Outline the Project Plan with children how to do the project. Consider:

- the scope of the project (see Project Options)
- the audience—such as families, veterans, PTA, or younger children
- identify the historical era the class would like to focus on and whether or not children want to tell a brief history of America through songs
- research needed: American folk songs, simple historical time line

Once a theme has been decided upon, have group members organize themselves and define tasks. All group work should be recorded in the project journal.

❸ EXPLORE MUSIC IDEAS

- Children should choose individual roles for the project, such as Musical Directors, Writers, and Set and Prop Managers.
- Depending on how the project is done, the class may be organized so that each group develops a song or a time in history.
- Children may look for song ideas in songbooks or use CDs, records, and audiocassettes as resources. They should consider both songs they know and ones they will need to learn.

Family members or friends who are able to play an instrument can become part of the production. Others may contribute songbooks and other resources.

CLASSROOM MANAGEMENT

You may want to have time set aside daily for a sing-along of songs the groups are learning.

 **For Students with Special Needs**

Children who speak English as a second language should be paired with fluent English-speaking partners who can provide extra help learning the folk songs.

CAREERS IN ART

Children should be aware of these music-related careers as they work on this project.

vocalist

musical theater performer

music director

arranger

composer

lyricist

❹ CREATE A THEME

Some themes that might be used are:

Patriotic: *Yankee Doodle, The Star-Spangled Banner, America the Beautiful, America*

Early Settler Days: *Go Tell Aunt Rhody, There's a Hole in the Bucket, Turkey in the Straw, Hush Little Baby*

Settling of the West: *Sweet Betsy from Pike, Clementine, Oh, Susanna, Home on the Range*

Coming of the Railroad: *I've Been Workin' on the Railroad, She'll Be Comin' Round the Mountain, John Henry, Rock Island Line, This Land Is Your Land*

- Using the copying master on page 37 as a planning guide, children should list their songs.

❺ REHEARSE AND REFINE

- Have children sing their songs into a tape recorder, and then play them back so they can listen to how they sound. Then they should note ways they can improve.
- Have at least one dress rehearsal before the performance and, if possible, videotape that rehearsal. Then have children critique one another's performances.

❻ PERFORM IT!

Some options for the performance include:

- performing for special groups such as veterans, PTA, and patriotic community groups
- videotaping the show and putting it in the school's media center so it can be checked out by study groups

Performance and Process Assessments

Review with children the project journals and their performances based on the goals set at the beginning of the project. Add personal evaluations and responses to the project journals.

✔ **For the Student**
  - How did the audience respond to your performance?
  - What did you learn about history and folk songs?

✔ **For the Teacher**
  - How effective were children's ideas and performances?
  - Were children able to understand the influence of historical events on music?

PERFORMING ARTS PROJECT

Folk Songs Tell a Story

Write and Draw About a Song

Pick a song and write its title on the line. Then write some of the words of the song. Next, write a sentence about the song and draw a picture that shows what the song tells.

Song Title _______________________

____

Words _______________________

____

____

This song is about _______________________

____

____

Zigzag Dancing

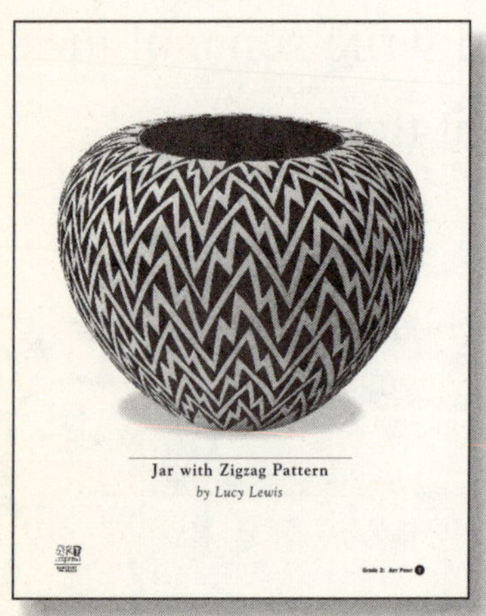

▲ **Art Print 7,** *Jar with zigzag pattern,* Lucy Lewis

OBJECTIVE: Children will explore linear movement, rhythms, and patterns and create a dance.

MATERIALS: *Art Print 7, Performing Arts Cassette:* "Arica," crayons or markers, sheets of unlined paper

TIPS AND TIME-SAVERS You may wish to have children rest after a session of movement activities. Choose soft music to set the mood as children rest, reflect, and get ready to write.

⊙ WARM-UP

Set the stage for exploring linear movement by having children draw lines on paper as they listen to a variety of musical selections with various rhythms. Use the *Performing Arts Cassette* or select other music. Then display *Art Print 7, Jar with zigzag pattern* and ask volunteers to describe what they see. Discuss any of the following questions:

- **Are any of the lines you made similar to those on the jar?**

- **Do you think the artist who made the jar was thinking about any special kind of music as she created her work? What music might that have been?**

⊙ DANCE ACTIVITY

Take children to an open area. Tell them they are going to follow imaginary lines on the floor as they move. Explain that those lines may be curved, straight, or zigzag like the lines on the jar. With music playing in the background, lead children in an exploration of linear movement. Then have volunteers take turns leading several small groups as they walk in lines near one another or cut through one another's lines. Remind children to keep an image in mind of the kind of line they are following. After the activity, have children return to their papers.

- **What are some words that tell about the kinds of lines your group made? Write them in a list.**

- **Draw the lines on paper that your group followed.**

- **Write about your favorite line to move in.**

Continue the activity by having children work with a partner. Mark an open area with starting and ending points. Encourage children to move from point to point, following any kind of line including straight. Have them recall for ideas the lines on the jar in *Art Print 7* and the lines they followed in their groups. Suggest that they use various ways to move, such as walk, hop, skip, gallop, creep, crawl, and scoot. After partners have experimented for a while, let them present their creative movement for the rest of the group.

◎ REFLECT

Have children gather in front of *Jar with zigzag pattern*. Play "Arica" in the background. Then discuss the following:

- **Now that you have moved in lines similar to those on the jar, do you see anything new as you look at it?**

- **What patterns do you see?**

- **What kinds of lines would you make on a jar?**

Informal Assessment

✔ Were children's movements appropriate and creative?

✔ Did children develop an understanding of linear movement?

ANIMAL STORIES Organize children into small groups. Ask each group to think of an animal they would like to portray. Then have them create a short story about that animal. They should use some of the linear movements they experimented with as they move their animals from place to place on stage. ■ GOAL: CREATIVE EXPRESSION

GOING UP OR DOWN Have children make up a melody that follows a line that they draw, or that follows one of the lines on the *Jar with zigzag pattern*. Children may interpret the pattern with either long or short sounds. Assure them that there is no correct melody; each child is free to make a personal interpretation. ■ GOAL: CREATIVE EXPRESSION

What's the Story?

▲ **Art Print 8,** *Le Pont du Gard,* Hubert Robert

OBJECTIVE: Children devise a story to tell based on the painting.

MATERIALS: *Art Print 8, Performing Arts Cassette:* "Allegro"

TIPS AND TIME-SAVERS You may wish to provide simple props such as hats, a map, binoculars or a homemade spyglass, or other props that will help children when they tell their story.

✆ WARM-UP

Display *Art Print 8, Le Pont du Gard,* and ask volunteers to describe and discuss what they see. Point out that what looks like a large bridge is an aqueduct, an ancient structure for carrying water from one place to another. Discuss any of the following:

- **Who are these people?**

- **Where do you think this aqueduct is?**

- **What do you think might happen next?**

✆ THEATER ACTIVITY

Discuss with children that storytelling is an ancient art. Tell them that many stories have been passed from one generation to the next by word of mouth rather than by being read. Explain that small groups will meet and plan a group story to tell. Organize children into groups or four or five. Then give them this story beginning: *Once upon a time, some people who lived near a river....* Ask these questions to help the groups get started:

- **What will happen next to the people? How can you tell this as a story?**

- **What actions can help you tell your story?**

Have children continue to brainstorm things that might happen to the people, such as where they might be traveling and what they might do when they get there. Allow time for each group to tell its story for the class. Point out the variety of ways each group told its story based on what they saw in the painting.

⊚ REFLECT

Once again, view the painting *Le Pont du Gard*. Play "Allegro" as children study the painting. Then discuss the following:

- **Now that you've told stories about the people, what do you notice about the painting that you didn't see before?**

- **What story do you think the artist wanted to tell when he painted this?**

Informal Assessment

✔ Were children able to capture the storytelling form?

✔ Were all children working toward the goal of performance?

WATER MUSIC Collect or make simple rhythm instruments. Have children make up a rhythm pattern and play it to accompany stories they create. For example, each time the people travel on the water to a new place, the same rhythm could be played. ■ **GOAL: CREATIVE EXPRESSION**

SLOW DANCE Have children create a dance about moving water or any detail they see in the painting. Then have them perform the dance in slow motion. ■ **GOAL: CREATIVE EXPRESSION**

Circus Clown Acts

Unit Project Overview: Children use a circus theme to pantomime feelings and emotions through clown acts.

MATERIALS

- *Performing Arts Cassette*
- mirror
- World Wide Web: *International Clown Hall of Fame* (http://digetal.net/ ~steref/clowns.html)
- videotape: *Circus Day* (SVE, 1995)

VOCABULARY CONCEPTS

You may wish to teach these **Glossary** words and concepts in context during the project.

acting
director
improvisation
expression
pantomime

CROSS-CURRICULAR CONNECTIONS

Fine Arts Theater, Music
Language Arts Reading, Writing, Listening, Speaking
Social Studies Social Participation, Feelings, Emotions
Math Time

PROJECT OBJECTIVES

Artistic Perception Move as people or characters children have observed.

Creative Expression Convey the emotional qualities of people or given characters through simple dramatizations.

Historical/Cultural Context Use contemporary culture as a basis for creative dramatic play.

Aesthetic Valuing Discuss the use of basic acting terminology, such as *projection* and *vocal* and *physical characterization* of self and others.

① WARM-UP

Choose one of the following activities:

- Invite volunteers to act out various emotions (happy, sad, surprised) as the class tries to guess what they are. Suggest that children think of an event to help them project the emotion. Some examples might be getting a new bike, not getting to go to a ball game, or winning a prize. Have children draw a happy face and write about an event that made them very happy, or sad, or surprised.

- Have partners experiment with the technique of "mirroring." You may want to practice some teacher-led group mirroring activities first. Then have partners practice simple mirror movements, such as tilting or turning their heads, while facing each other. Then try more complex mirroring such as making a sandwich or other activities that involve several steps.

Have children discuss the following ideas and record their responses in their project journals.

- **Write about an event that involved a lot of emotion.**
- **How can you project feelings and emotions when you act out an event?**

❷ PLAN THE PROJECT

Set Goals Explain to children that they will create and perform a circus clown's act. Help children with the following project goals:

- create, remember, and perform a circus clown's act
- work with a partner on the act
- present a cohesive, meaningful performance

Outline the Project Plan with children how to do the project. Consider the following:

- the scope of the project (see Project Options)
- the intended audience—parents, younger or older children
- what each act will be about
- the research that will need to be done

Also, the group needs to make some decisions about the performance, such as whether to have an intermission and refreshments. Advertising should also be considered and possibly ticket sales (with the money going to a worthy cause). All group work can be recorded in the project journal.

❸ EXPLORE THEATER IDEAS

- Children should choose classmates to assist with the production. It might be a good idea to have a Director who will take the role of the Ring master and who will decide the order of the acts. Also, several people will be needed to work on the set and costumes, as well as a music coordinator.
- Partners should begin identifying the act they will perform.
- Have children experiment with different ideas, such as a happy clown with a trained dog, a lady clown with a crying baby, or worried clown firefighters. This might be a good time to view a circus movie or videotapes about clowns or mimes.

- Without costumes, props, or a set, have children create and perform circus clown acts. **SIMPLE**

- Help children develop a complete circus to go with the clown acts. There could be lion tamers, dancing bears, and equestrian acts. This may also be done with a cultural theme in mind since the circus is a performance medium common to many countries. **ELABORATE**

Contact parents and check the yellow pages to find one or more clowns who can visit the class. Enlist their support to help children with their performances.

❹ CREATE THE ACTS

- As children begin to work on their circus clown acts, have them try out their material on one another and provide feedback.
- Use the copying master on page 45, and have children create a list of acts, performers, and music for everyone in the show.
- Children should decide on costumes and begin making or assembling them. Many clown costumes use oversized clothes, so old adult clothing is always a good source.
- The stage or area where the acts will take place should now have the beginnings of the stage decorations or backdrop.
- Music to accompany each act should now be in place.

❺ REHEARSE AND REFINE

- Children should rehearse their performances and the Ring master should make decisions about the performing order.
- Have at least one student-timed dress rehearsal to run through all the acts from beginning to end.
- Children who are not performing can help coordinate the audio needs and the prop management, and set up for the performing acts.

❻ PERFORM IT!

Some options for the performance include:
- videotaping the performance so it can be shown to people in nursing homes or elder-care facilities
- arranging for an outdoor or "touring" performance

Performance and Process Assessments

Review with children the project journals and their performances based on the goals set at the beginning of the project. Encourage children to add personal evaluations and responses to the project journals.

✔ **For the Student**
- How did my contribution help the overall performance?
- How did projection help my performance?

✔ **For the Teacher**
- How effective were children in portraying feelings and emotions? Which children effectively used projection techniques?
- In what way did the group's planning efforts benefit the final performance?

Name _______________________________

Circus Clown Acts

Setting a Lineup for a Show

Fill in the boxes to help organize the acts.

Act Number _______________________________

Name of the Act _______________________________

____

Performers _______________________________

____

____

Music _______________________________

Act Number _______________________________

Name of the Act _______________________________

____

Performers _______________________________

____

____

Music _______________________________

Let's Dance

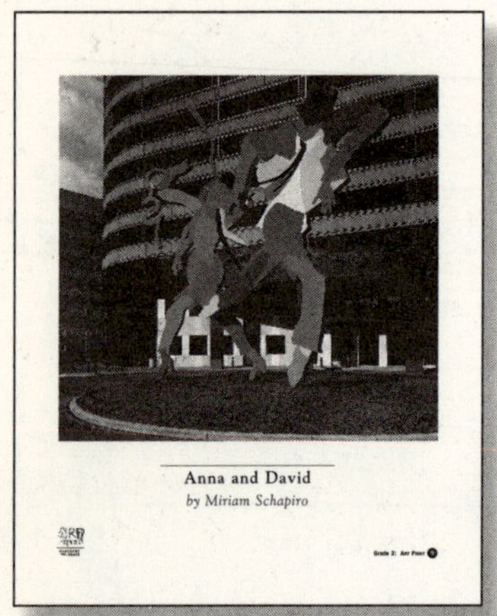

▲ **Art Print 9,** *Anna and David,*
Miriam Schapiro

OBJECTIVE: Children experiment with some simple, rhythmic dance steps.

MATERIALS: *Art Print 9, Performing Arts Cassette:* "Lullaby," "Dancin' in Rhythm," "You're in Love, Charlie Brown"

TIPS AND TIME-SAVERS
Continuously praise and encourage children's movement explorations. Your acceptance of what they are doing will open the door for them to try more movement experiments and will build self-esteem.

⊚ WARM-UP

Play "Dancin' in Rhythm" to create a high-energy feeling. Then display *Art Print 9, Anna and David.* Identify the name of the piece and the sculptor for children. Ask for volunteers to describe what they see. Have a discussion based on the following questions:

- **What words or phrases can you use to describe *Anna and David*?**

- **How do you think Anna and David feel?**

- **Do you think we are seeing them in the morning or at night? Why?**

- **What message do you think the sculptor is giving to people who view *Anna and David*?**

- **Why do you think the sculptor chose such bright colors for her work?**

⊚ DANCE ACTIVITY

Organize children into groups of three or four. Have the group members line up side by side. Begin playing a slow-tempo song, such as "Lullaby" or one from your own sources. Have children link arms or hold hands and try a few rhythmic moves as a group while they keep time with the music. For example, have them sway from side to side or have them take a side step to the right and then a side step to the left. Then have them do a step up and a step back. Explain that when they are moving over and over in the same pattern, they are moving in rhythm.

Now play a faster-tempo song such as "You're in Love, Charlie Brown" from the *Performing Arts Cassette.* Let children experiment with the same moves but now at a somewhat faster tempo.

Encourage children to experiment with other rhythmic movements in their groups, such as four steps up and clap, or four steps back and clap.

Children may be interested in trying a leap as Anna and David are doing in *Art Print 9*. Suggest that they do a slightly lower-level leap at first and then experiment to see how high they can go.

Have each group choose one of the songs and perform their dance steps for others. Discuss with children how they used the rhythm of the music to help them move together.

REFLECT

Gather children in front of *Art Print 9, Anna and David,* and play "Dancin' in Rhythm" in the background. Have children study the sculpture as they listen to the music. Then discuss the following:

- **Now that you've done some dancing, what do think of the action in the sculpture?**

- **How did the sculpture help you with your dancing? What did you think about when you danced?**

Informal Assessment

✔ Were children able to move and encourage each other's dancing?

✔ Did a group leader seem to emerge, or did members of the group contribute equally in deciding the dance movements?

FIND THE RHYTHM Have children sing some familiar clapping songs. Two to try are "Bingo" and "My Hat, It Has Three Corners." Sing a song once, then repeat the song again and again, each time leaving out one more word and substituting a clap for the word. Finally, children will not be singing at all, but just clapping the rhythm of the song. ■ **GOAL: HISTORICAL/CULTURAL CONTEXT**

LET'S TALK Have children create a dialogue for Anna and David. Have them discuss with a partner what the two might be saying to each other. They might be talking about where they are going, how they feel, or what they are going to do. ■ **GOAL: CREATIVE EXPRESSION**

Listen to This

▲ Art Print 10, *Mother and Child*, Mary Cassatt

OBJECTIVE: Children explore feelings and moods in music.

MATERIALS: *Art Print 10, Performing Arts Cassette:* "Lullaby," tape recorder

TIPS AND TIME-SAVERS When teaching children a new song, first read or say the song phrase by phrase. Sing the words and music of the song a small section at a time, and have children repeat after you. Then sing the whole song together.

◎ WARM-UP

Write the words *happy, sad,* and *angry* on separate slips of paper. Put the slips into a box or jar. Then, with children, list the names of some songs they know, such as "Clementine," "Oh, Where, Oh Where Has My Little Dog Gone?" or "If You're Happy and You Know It." Sing one of the songs. Then have a volunteer or group draw one of the slips out, and have the class sing the song again in a way that expresses the feeling on the slip. Discuss how the mood or feeling of the song changed.

Display *Mother and Child* and discuss any of the following:

- **How do you think the child feels?**

- **What do you think the mother is thinking about?**

- **What kind of mood does the whole painting show?**

◎ MUSIC ACTIVITY

Have children tape-record singing a song. Use a song they listed in the Warm-Up or one of the others they know. Have them sing at different tempos; in fact, have them exaggerate the tempos by singing very, very fast and then very, very slow. Play back the tape, and have children listen to the differences and discuss the changes.

- **What mood or feeling do you hear or feel when people sing fast?**

- **What is the mood or feeling you hear in your slow song?**

- **What else could you do to make a song show a feeling or mood?**

Have children continue experimenting with music and mood by having them think of some ways to add to or exaggerate the mood of the songs. For example, ask them how they can make a scary song scarier. They may use some rhythm band instruments or create other sound effects, such as scraping or scratching. A wind sound can be made by using voices, and the sound of horses' hooves can be made by "clucking" one's tongue or using wood blocks. Allow children to try out some of their ideas, tape-record them, and play their finished music for themselves and others to enjoy.

⊚ REFLECT

Gather children in a group and display *Art Print 10*. Play "Lullaby," and have children listen to the song as they study the painting. Then discuss the following questions:

- **What do you like or dislike about this painting?**
- **What kind of a mood are you in as you look at this painting? What does the music do to your mood?**
- **How would you describe this painting to someone?**

Informal Assessment

✔ Did children understand the differences in moods?

✔ Could children use what they learned about mood to create moods or feelings with music and sounds?

CREATE A MOOD Have children recite a short poem they know and pretend they are the mother or the child in the painting. Then have them recite the poem as if they were an older brother or sister.
■ **GOAL: CREATIVE EXPRESSION**

DANCE WITH FEELING
Mark sections of the floor into four squares labeled *happy, sad, scared, surprised*. Organize four groups and place a group in each square. Have children begin to dance when the music starts. When the music stops, children stop and assume a dance pose that conveys the feeling named in their square. Rotate the groups through each square. ■ **GOAL: CREATIVE EXPRESSION**

Circle Dancing

Unit Project Overview: Children make up circle dances and perform them for an audience.

- *Performing Arts Cassette* or other recorded music with a lively beat for dancing
- videotape: *Dance with Us,* Ezmiar Productions, Newberry, FL, 1992

VOCABULARY CONCEPTS

You may wish to teach these **Glossary** words and concepts in context during the project.

> **choreography**
> **folk dance**
> **social dance**

CROSS-CURRICULAR CONNECTIONS

Fine Arts Dance, Music
Math Shapes, Directions, Counting
Social Studies Cultures, Cultural Dances
Language Arts Listening, Speaking, Reading, Writing

PROJECT OBJECTIVES

Artistic Perception Choose and perform dance movements based on circular moves. Teach the dance to others.

Creative Expression Create circular dance patterns using chosen rhythms and tempos.

Historical/Cultural Context Watch a videotape or live performance of a cultural circle dance.

Aesthetic Valuing Describe the movements of others and compare with one's own dance.

❶ WARM-UP

Choose one of the following activities:

- With children, form a large circle holding hands. Help children sing "The Ants Go Marching" or another familiar song with a strong beat. Begin circling to the right. Release your left hand and begin to coil inward slowly, leading children to form an ever-tightening circle. When the circle is as tight as it can be, turn and lead children in the opposite direction. The outgoing children will pass children following the incoming spiral. At the end, everyone will be back in place in a large circle.

- Have children view a live or videotaped performance of dances. Discuss how the dancers move. Have children notice in which directions the dancers are moving and whether they are in a line or in a circle. Have children share some ideas about a group dance they might do.

Have children discuss the following ideas and record responses in their project journals.

- **What is a way to help remember right and left?**
- **How can you use rhythm to help with the dance?**

❷ PLAN THE PROJECT

Set Goals Explain to children that they are going to make up a circle dance and perform it for others. Help children with the following project goals:
- create, remember, and perform a dance sequence
- dance with a group, synchronizing moves
- produce a meaningful, cohesive performance

Outline the Project Plan with children how to do the project. Consider:
- the scope of the project (see Project Options)
- the audience—such as families or younger children
- whether the class would like to perform as one large group or several smaller ones
- the research needed: circle dances, traditional dances of cultural groups

❸ EXPLORE DANCE IDEAS

- Children should choose individual roles for the project, such as Dance Leader, Dancers, and Planner.

- Children should choose music to accompany their dances. They may want to experiment first with different rhythms and tempos as they try out their dances.

- Without costumes, props, or set pieces, have children create and perform a circle dance to music for class-mates. **SIMPLE**

- Wearing costumes and with props and set pieces, children can create and perform circle dances to music as part of a dance festival. **ELABORATE**

Invite parent dancers or cultural dance groups to visit the class. Many will have special costumes to wear and share with children. Some may be willing to teach dances to children.

CLASSROOM MANAGEMENT

Ask one or two children to demonstrate a particularly creative movement that you observe. Have others watch and then try working similar movements into their dances.

 **For Students with Special Needs**

Some children may need to use shorter dance phrases and have fewer of them to sequence.

CAREERS IN ART

Children should be aware of these dance-related careers as they work on this project.

choreographer

folk/ethnic dancer

dance instructor

❹ CREATE A DANCE

- As children make up their dances, have each child perform the dance, in stages, for other group members. Lead children to identify any parts of the dance that may not be working, and help them make changes.
- Using the copying master on page 53 as a guide for notating movements, children can record dance movements so they will remember them for rehearsals.
- Children should decide on any costumes they want to use and begin gathering or making them.

❺ REHEARSE AND REFINE

- Children rehearse the performance, with the whole class or the groups performing in order.
- Have at least one dress rehearsal to go through the dance performances.
- Children who are not performing may help coordinate the groups' dances and the audio and prop needs, invite the audience, and write and make the programs for the performance.

❻ PERFORM IT!

Some options for the performance include:
- videotaping the performance so it can be shared with other classes or dance groups
- setting up at a local community festival which may include performances by dance groups

Performance and Process Assessments

Review with children the project journals and their performances based on the goals set at the beginning of the project. Encourage children to add personal evaluations and responses to the project journals.

✔ **For the Student**
- Compare your dance with the dances of others. What was good about your dance? What was good about theirs?
- How did knowing about rhythm, movement, and circles help with your dancing?

✔ **For the Teacher**
- Were children able to use a variety of circular moves in their dances, or did they safely stick to only one or two?
- How well did the Dance Leaders function?

Name _______________________________

Circle Dancing

Planning a Dance

When you plan a dance, you should write your plan for it.
You may use this sheet as a guide. You can write, draw, and
label the plan using these symbols or make up some of your
own to show your dance.

▼　Use this for a person.
→　Use this to show the direction the dancers move.
◆　Use this to show when the dancers stop or stand.
✖　Use this to show when the dancers cross.
●　Use this to show when the dancers form a circle.

Example

▼ ▼ ▼ ▼ ● →　(4 people circle right)

Your notes here:

____

____

____

____

____

Who Is This?

Las Meninas
by Diego Velázquez

▲ **Art Print 11,** *Las Meninas,*
Diego Velázquez

OBJECTIVE: Children explore characterization through an interview.

MATERIALS: *Art Print 11, Performing Arts Cassette:* "Vals no. 3," storybooks, video: Encyclopedia Britannica Education Corporation: Familiar Tales Around the World series, "Hansel and Gretel" or similar tale

CLASSROOM MANAGEMENT
Make a list of storybook characters before you begin the theater activity.

◉ WARM-UP

Play some of "Vals no. 3" to set the mood for viewing *Las Meninas*. Explain to children that in the painting the young girl, a royal princess, is having her portrait painted. Discuss details about who each character in the painting might be, including the artist who added himself as the "portrait painter." Tell students that *las meninas* means "the maids."

- **What do you think the artist in the painting is thinking?**

- **What are "the maids" doing?**

- **Where do you think this scene might be?**

◉ THEATER ACTIVITY

Show a storybook video or display and discuss some familiar storybooks. Explain to children that some of them are going to portray some storybook characters and that others are going to try to guess who they are by their actions. Begin by whispering the name of a storybook character to one child. Allow the child a minute or two to "get into character." At your signal the child begins acting as the character would act. The group tries to guess who that character is by interviewing him or her. To help identify the character, they may ask charades-type questions similar to the following:

- **Is your character a boy or a girl? Young or old? Small or large?**

- **Is your character usually alone or mostly with others?**

When the character is guessed, allow some time for discussion about the way in which the characterization was done. For example, children could discuss how they were able to guess the character portrayed (by the way the character walked, smiled, and so on). Continue by giving each member of the group the opportunity to become a storybook character. Then have children work with a partner to improve and refine their characterizations. Have some of the portrayals replayed for the group. Ask the class what made the character easy or hard to identify. Ask the characters to tell whether it was easy or hard to portray someone else.

◉ REFLECT

Gather the class for another look at *Art Print 11, Las Meninas*. Play "Vals no. 3" in the background as children study the print. Ask volunteers to tell if they are now able to understand more about what each character is doing and why. Then discuss the following:

- **Why do you think the young girl has the maids and the dog with her?**

- **What kind of life do you think the young girl has?**

- **How do you think she treats her maids? Why do you think so?**

- **How do you think the people in the painting walk and talk?**

- **What would you say to the artist who is painting the girl's portrait?**

Informal Assessment

✔ Were children able to assume many of the characteristics of the storybook characters?

✔ Are children able to understand that characters have motivations for their actions?

THEIR SONG Have children listen to several musical selections and decide on one they think best portrays a certain character. Have children share why they chose that music. ■ GOAL: AESTHETIC VALUING

"BECOMING" DANCE Have children experiment with dance movements to portray characters in certain situations, such as Goldilocks delivering pizza to the three bears or the Gingerbread Boy as a canoeist paddling down a river. ■ GOAL: CREATIVE EXPRESSION

New Words for an Old Song

▲ *Art Print 12, France,* Elliot Erwitt

OBJECTIVE: With children, rewrite the words of a familiar song. Then sing the new song.

MATERIALS: *Art Print 12, Performing Arts Cassette:* "You're in Love, Charlie Brown"

TIPS AND TIME-SAVERS You may wish to point out that the bicycle in the photograph is not built for two and that it's really not a good idea to ride double, even when cars are not present.

⊚ WARM-UP

Display *Art Print 12, France,* tell children the name, and explain that France is a country in Europe. Discuss with children the following questions:

- **Who do you think the child on the bicycle is looking at?**

- **What are some things that tell you that this photograph was taken in France?**

- **How is the child in the photograph like you?**

⊚ MUSIC ACTIVITY

Ask children to tell how the people in the photograph are traveling and to speculate about where they have been. Discuss how children get around where they live and what they do to help their families—for example, carrying groceries or shopping. Talk about the bicycle as a mode of transportation. Sing an old favorite bicycle song, "A Bicycle Built for Two" ("Daisy, Daisy").

Explain that you are going to work with the class to think of some new words for an old song. As children begin to think of new words to the song, write them on the board or on chart paper as children dictate them. Allow time for rewriting and adjusting words to fit the melody. When all the words are complete, sing your new song.

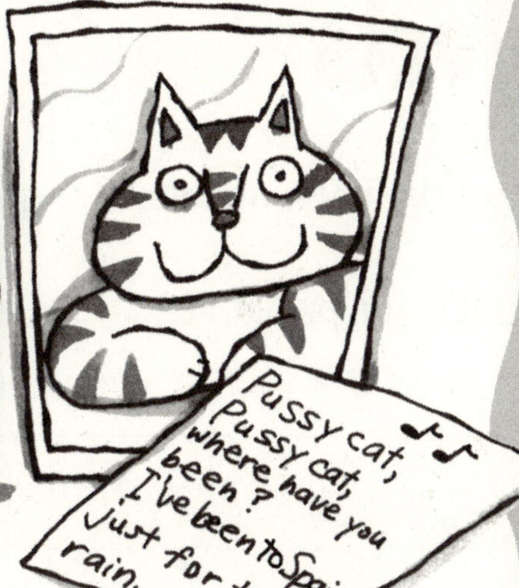

Continue by singing other songs and writing new words for them. Have children take photographs or find or draw pictures to go with their songs. Help children plan a way to share these songs with others in their school or in their community.

⊚ REFLECT

Gather children in front of *France*. Play "You're in Love, Charlie Brown." Ask children to listen closely to the rhythm of the song. Compare it to the rhythm of a bicycle being pedaled.

- **What do you notice about the child that is different from you or the same as you?**

- **Why do you think the photographer took this picture?**

- **What would you like to take a picture of?**

Informal Assessment

✔ Were children able to compare their life with the lives of others?

✔ Were children able to contribute to the rewriting of the song?

CIRCLING AROUND Have children perform a circle dance as they sing songs. They should hold hands and dance to the right on the verse of the song and then dance to the left on the song's chorus. They can dance using a variety of steps as they move around in a circle. ■ GOAL: CREATIVE EXPRESSION

DRAMATIZE THE PHOTOGRAPH Have partners role-play the conversation the child and the man might be having. Have them present their dialogues to the class. ■ GOAL: CREATIVE EXPRESSION

Group/Self-Assessment for Unit Projects

Think about your project work. Then answer the questions.

What do you like best about your project?

____

____

____

What is the most difficult part of your project?

____

____

____

What would you like to change? Explain or draw a picture.

____

____

____

Peer Assessment for Unit Projects

Think about the performance you watched.

Did you enjoy the performance? Why or why not?

____

____

____

What was your favorite part? Explain or draw a picture.

____

____

____

What special things did the performers do?

____

____

____

Glossary of Performing Arts Terms

ACTING The process by which an individual uses his or her body, mind, voice, and emotions to interpret the role of a character.

ACTION The sense of forward movement created by the events of a play and the motivations of its characters.

ACTOR A person who acts the part of a character in a play.

AUDIENCE Any person or group watching or listening to a performance, viewing art, or reading a written work.

AXIAL MOVEMENT Movement of body parts around the axis of the body—for example, twisting, reaching, and pivoting—which is anchored to one spot.

BACKSTAGE The area offstage that includes the dressing rooms and storage places for props and scenery.

BALLET A classical dance form that originated in the Renaissance courts of Europe. Steps and body positions were set in the 1600s. The Romantic ballet, as it is known today, began in the 1800s, led by Jules Perrot in France, August Bournonville in Denmark, and Marius Petipa in Russia. Further development was the work of Michel Fokine (Russia); Kenneth MacMillan and Anthony Tudor (England); and George Balanchine, Jerome Robbins, and Arthur Mitchell (United States).

BAND A group of musicians who play instruments together.

BAROQUE MUSIC An exuberant and emotional style of music that was developed in Europe between about 1600 and 1750. It is exemplified in the operas of Claudio Monteverdi and in the concertos of Johann Sebastian Bach and Antonio Vivaldi.

BEAT The basic unit of time in music.

BLOCKING, STAGING The positions (center stage, downstage, upstage, stage right, stage left) and movements of the actors on the stage that are designed to focus the audience's attention on the important points of action.

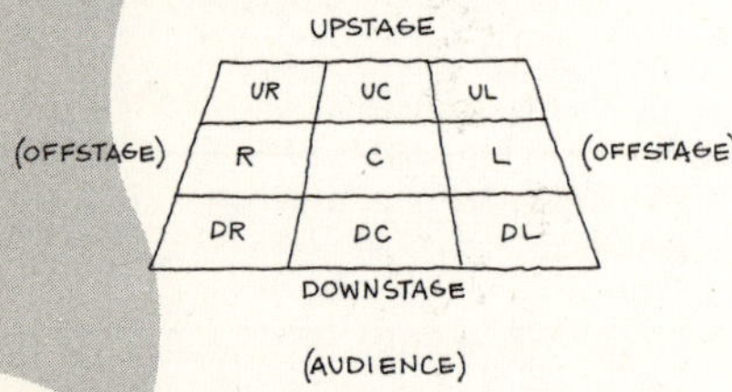

BRASS FAMILY A group of metal instruments, such as the trumpet, that are blown into.

CALL-AND-RESPONSE A musical form in which one performer is echoed or answered by another or by a group. This also occurs with dance movements. It is associated with African music and dance.

CAST All of the actors in a performance.

CHARACTER A person in a play whose physical, mental, and emotional characteristics are portrayed by an actor.

CHORD A combination of three or more tones sounded at once.

CHOREOGRAPHER A person who composes dances.

CHOREOGRAPHY The art of composing dances.

CLASSICAL MUSIC 1. Art music of any culture, as distinguished from folk or popular music or jazz. 2. European music of the classical period, from about 1750 to 1825, for example, music by Haydn, Mozart, and Beethoven.

CONFLICT The problem that sets up the action and must be resolved by the end of the play.

CONTEMPORARY Music or other art marked by characteristics of the present period.

COSTUME Clothing worn by a performer to enhance interpretation of his or her character.

CREATIVE DRAMA An improvisation in which participants are guided by a leader to imagine a situation and react to it.

CREATIVE MOVEMENT, CREATIVE DANCE, OR MOVEMENT EXPLORATION Dance based on improvisation, usually to express an emotion, a theme, or a movement element such as time, force, or space.

DANCE 1. A work of movement that is unified in the manner of a poem, a piece of music, a play, or a painting. It has structure and a purpose or a set of movement themes. It is often accompanied by music. 2. The field of study of expressive movement and its place in society in the past and present. It includes methods of choreography and performance and other related studies.

DANCE NOTATION A system of recording dance movements. Best known are Benesh notation and Laban notation; however, recent technology has made videotape the most popular method of recording dance.

DANCE STYLE 1. An individual performer's way of performing any kind of dance. 2. A particular dance technique, such as that taught at the Vaganova Choreographic Institute in Russia; a historical period of dance, such as Romantic ballet (1880s) or early modern dance (1900 to 1940).

DANCE TYPE (GENRE) Genres include ballet, modern, tap, jazz, Indonesian, and East Indian. Each kind of dance has its own technique, system, vocabulary, form, and method of performance.

DIALOGUE The words spoken by actors as the speech of their characters.

DIRECTOR The director of a performance who coordinates all aspects of the production.

DRAMA 1. A play written to be performed by actors. 2. The study of writing and performing plays.

DYNAMICS 1. The volume of sound. 2. The marks used to indicate how loudly or softly music is to be performed.

ELEMENTS OF DANCE The components used to create dance. These components are *force/energy, space,* and *time.*

ELEMENTS OF MUSIC The components used to create works of music. These components are *dynamics, form, harmony, pitch, rhythm, tempo, texture,* and *timbre.*

ELEMENTS OF THEATER The components used to create works of theater. These components are *character, dialogue, plot,* and *theme.*

ENSEMBLE A group of performers able to work together to present a production.

ENTERTAINMENT OR COMMERCIAL DANCE An American type of dance—often employing jazz, tap, ballet, and modern dance—used in Broadway musicals, film, television, and music videos.

EXPRESSION A quality of a composition or performance that produces an emotional effect.

FOLK DANCE Dance connected with a country's traditions.

FOLK MUSIC, FOLK SONG Traditional music that has been passed from generation to generation.

FORCE/ENERGY This dance element involves the release of potential energy into kinetic energy. Body weight and gravity affect the motion of the dancers through space.

FORM The structure of a piece of music, achieved through the use of techniques such as repetition, contrast, unity, and variety to organize musical ideas.

FORMAL PRODUCTION The staging of a theatrical work for presentation for an audience. It also refers to music and dance.

GREEK THEATER The term usually refers to the style of theater of ancient Greece, developed in the fifth century B.C.

HARMONY The blending of two or more tones sounded simultaneously; a progression of chords.

IMPROVISATION The spontaneous creation of movement, music, or a character or scene.

INFORMAL PRODUCTION The exploration of a theatrical work in a setting geared to experimentation. It also refers to music and dance.

INSTRUMENT A device used to produce musical sounds, such as a violin or a saxophone.

JAZZ A style of music that originated in the American South with African Americans; it has strong rhythm, improvisation, and syncopation. Influential jazz musicians include Scott Joplin, Louis Armstrong, Duke Ellington, and Billie Holiday.

JAZZ DANCE Dance characterized by movement isolations and complex rhythms. Jazz dance grew from the music of African American ragtime, jazz, spirituals, blues, and work songs. Its rhythms and gestures also show East Indian, gypsy, Spanish, Caribbean, and South American influences.

KINESTHETIC AWARENESS Conscious perception of movement. Kinesthetic awareness is fostered in dance education.

LOCOMOTOR MOVEMENT The movement of the body through space. It may be described by type of movement, such as *walk, run, leap,* or *skip.*

MELODY A succession of musical tones in a rhythmic pattern.

MIDI (Musical Instrument Digital Interface) A standardized "language" that allows electronic instruments to communicate with one another and with a computer.

MODERN DANCE A twentieth-century dance genre that began by breaking away from the formal steps and positions of ballet to produce a more expressive movement. It was first explored by American Isadora Duncan in Europe and by Mary Wigman and Rudolph Laban in Germany. Innovators in the United States were Ruth St. Denis, Ted Shawn, Martha Graham, Doris Humphrey, and Charles Weidman.

MONOLOGUE A dramatic sketch performed by one person.

MOTIF A distinctive gesture used at recurring intervals to unify dance ideas.

NARRATOR Someone who tells a story or outlines a presentation or play for an audience.

NOTATION The methods used to record music, dance, or directions for staged productions.

ORCHESTRA A large group of musicians playing together, usually for a formal presentation.

PANTOMIME Using movement and gesture to convey an idea, an emotion, or a character without using the voice.

PERCUSSION FAMILY A group of instruments, such as drums, that are struck or shaken.

PERFORMANCE MEDIA Media via which stories can be presented. They may include stage, film or videotape, television, radio, audio recording, and computer.

PHRASE A music or dance idea comparable to a sentence or a phrase in language.

PITCH The highness or lowness of a sound, determined by the frequency of the vibration producing it.

PLAY A story that is acted out for an audience. The characters' parts are written in script form for actors to follow.

PLOT The sequence of events that tells what happens in a play. It includes the problem the characters face, how they work to solve it, and how the problem is resolved.

POPULAR DANCE Contemporary dance prevalent at a particular time, for example, the jitterbug, the twist, or hip-hop.

POSTMODERN DANCE A type of dance introduced by Merce Cunningham that emerged in the 1960s. The use of pedestrian gesture and minimalism is characteristic of this type of dance; it is exemplified by Yvonne Ranier, Trisha Brown, Steve Paxton, and Rudy Perez.

PROP, PROPERTY Any object used to help make the character or setting believable.

RHYTHM An organized pattern of pulses or beats. It may be regular or irregular and may involve music or simply sounds made by the human body, such as foot stomps, heartbeats, or breath.

RITUAL DANCE A type of dance connected with the religious or traditional ceremonies of a particular culture.

ROLE The part of a character in a play. It is written by the playwright and interpreted by the actor.

ROLE PLAYING Improvising action and dialogue to portray a given situation, for example, a telephone conversation.

ROUND A melody started at different times by two or more musicians, who sing or play it together. This term can also refer to dance.

SCENE 1. A short incident that is part of a longer play. 2. The location of the action.

SCENERY Backdrops and furnishings that create for the audience the setting of the play's story.

SCRIPT The written dialogue, description, and directions for a play.

SET The physical setting, created by scenery and furniture, for the action of a play.

SETTING The time and place of the action of the play.

SHADOW PLAY, SHADOW DANCE A drama in which actors perform with a light source behind them and a screen (possibly a bedsheet) in front of them, so that the audience sees only their silhouettes on the screen.

SHAPE An aspect of space that involves the line of the body, affecting movement. Shape can be symmetrical or asymmetrical, open or closed, jagged or smooth.

SOCIAL DANCE A dance usually done with others in a social setting, such as ballroom dancing and square dancing.

SOUND EFFECTS Sound that imitates something real in a presentation, such as a play, a radio show, or a movie.

SPACE As an element of dance, the space surrounding the body in all directions. The use of space includes shape, direction, path, range, and level of movement.

STAFF A set of five horizontal lines on and around which musical notes are written.

STAGE Any place used for presenting shows to an audience.

STAGECRAFT The knowledge and skills required to handle the physical aspects of a production, such as scenery, props, lights, and sound.

STORYBOARD A graphic, visual outline of the sequence of events in a performance, such as an improvisation, a play, a film, or a television drama.

STORYTELLER A person who passes on a story by oral tradition; a person who dramatically tells a story rather than reading it.

STRING FAMILY A group of instruments, such as the violin, that are played by rubbing a bow against strings.

SYNCOPATION The temporary displacement of the regular beat.

TAP DANCE A type of dance based on rhythmic footwork, with roots in African American dance and Irish and English clogging traditions. Some leading performers and choreographers of tap dancing have been Bill "Bojangles" Robinson, Gregory Hines, Fred Astaire, and Gene Kelly.

TECHNIQUE The skills an artist must acquire for performing.

TEMPO The rate of speed of the music, based on the beat.

TEXTURE A pattern of musical sound created by tones or lines played or sung together. The thickness or thinness of sound is determined by the number of voices or instruments heard at one time.

THEATER Art that is focused toward the formal presentation of a scripted play. It includes acting, directing, designing, managing, and other technical tasks.

THEME The idea that is the focus of a composition.

TIMBRE The quality of tone produced by a particular voice or instrument.

TIME An element of dance involving rhythm, phrasing, tempo, accent, and duration. Time can be measured by music.

TONE 1. A particular pitch. 2. A musical note. 3. The quality of a sound. 4. The timbre of a particular instrument or voice.

VISUALIZATION A mental image of something that one creates in the mind's eye.

WOODWIND FAMILY A group of wind instruments, such as the clarinet and the flute, on which sound is produced by vibrating one or two reeds in the mouthpiece or by the passing of air over a mouth hole.

Cross-Curricular Connections

		Reading/ Literature	Language Arts/Writing	Social Studies
PERFORMING ARTS PROJECTS				
THEATER	**Unit 1:** Who I Want to Be	✔	✔	✔
MUSIC	**Unit 2:** Rhythm Band	✔	✔	✔
DANCE	**Unit 3:** Space Explorers Dance	✔	✔	✔
MUSIC	**Unit 4:** Folk Songs Tell a Story	✔	✔	✔
THEATER	**Unit 5:** Circus Clown Acts	✔	✔	✔
DANCE	**Unit 6:** Circle Dancing	✔	✔	✔
ART PRINT/PERFORMING ARTS ACTIVITIES				
MUSIC	*Art Print 1: The Family* Sounds for Everyone			✔
DANCE	*Art Print 2: Maudell Sleet's Magic Garden* From Seed to Flower		✔	
THEATER	*Art Print 3: Harvest at La Crau* Working the Land			✔
DANCE	*Art Print 4: Sketches of Cats* Move Like a Cat	✔		
MUSIC	*Art Print 5: Home Place* My Kind of Music	✔	✔	✔
THEATER	*Art Print 6: The Country School* When the Bell Rings			✔
DANCE	*Art Print 7: Jar with zigzag pattern* Zigzag Dancing	✔	✔	
THEATER	*Art Print 8: Le Pont du Gard* What's the Story?	✔		✔
DANCE	*Art Print 9: Anna and David* Let's Dance		✔	✔
MUSIC	*Art Print 10: Mother and Child* Listen to This	✔		✔
THEATER	*Art Print 11: Las Meninas* Who Is This?	✔		✔
MUSIC	*Art Print 12: France* New Words for an Old Song	✔	✔	✔

Science	Math	Fine Arts	Health/Physical Education
PERFORMING ARTS PROJECTS			
	✔	✔	
✔	✔	✔	
✔	✔	✔	✔
	✔	✔	
	✔	✔	
	✔	✔	✔
ART PRINT/PERFORMING ARTS ACTIVITIES			
✔		✔	✔
✔		✔	✔
		✔	✔
✔		✔	✔
	✔	✔	✔
	✔	✔	✔
✔	✔	✔	✔
✔	✔	✔	✔
		✔	✔
✔	✔	✔	✔
		✔	✔
	✔	✔	✔

Resources for the Performing Arts

BOOKS

Acting & Theatre by Cheryl Evans and Lucy Smith. EDC Publishing, 1992.

Drama for Learning by Dorothy Heathcote and Gavin Bolton. Heinemann, 1995.

Ella Jenkins' This Is Rhythm by Ella Jenkins. Sing Out Corporation, 1993.

The Good Apple Guide to Creative Drama by Kathy U. Foley, Mara Lud, Carol Power. Good Apple, 1981.

Great Composers by Piero Ventura. G.P. Putnam's Sons, 1988.

A Handbook of Creative Dance and Drama by Alison Lee. Heinemann, 1985.

Hands Around the World: 365 Ways to Build Cultural Awareness & Global Respect by Susan Milord. Williamson Publishing, 1992.

The Incredible Indoor Games Book by Bob Gregson. Fearon, 1982.

International Playtime by Wayne E. Nelson and Henry Glass. Fearon, 1992.

Jazz: History, Instruments, Musicians, Recordings by John Fordham. Dorling Kindersley, 1993.

Kids Make Music by Avery Hart and Paul Mantell. Williamson Publishing, 1993.

Making Music: Six Instruments You Can Create by Eddie Herschel Oates. HarperCollins, 1995.

Open Ears: Musical Adventures for a New Generation, edited by Sara deBeer. Ellipsis Kids..., 1995.

Putting on a Play: A Guide to Writing and Producing Neighborhood Drama by Susan and Stephen Judy. Scribner's, 1982.

Theater Games for the Classroom by Viola Spolin. Northwestern University Press, 1986.

We All Go Together: Creative Activities for Children to Use with Multicultural Folksongs by Doug Lipman. Oryx Press, 1994.

The Young People's Book of Music by Keith Spence. Millbrook. Aladdin Books, 1993.

ArtsEdge: The National Arts and Information Network:
http://artsedge.kennedycenter.org/artsedge.html

Heinemann Arts Subject Guide:
http://www.reedbooks.com.au/heinemann/subject/art.html

The Improv Page:
http://sunee.uwaterloo.ca/~broehl/improv/index.html

Marsalis on Music:
http://www.wnet.org.mom/index.html

STOMP:
http://www.usinteractive.com/stomp/home.html

Yahooligans Art Soup:
http://www.yahooligans.com/Art_Soup/

SOFTWARE

Dr. T's Sing-Along CD (Scholastic) Grades 1-5 (MAC/WIN CD)

Hollywood (Theatrix Interactive) Grade 4 up (MAC/WIN CD)

Julliard Music Adventure (Theatrix Interactive) Grade 4 up (MAC/WIN CD)

Kid Riffs CD (IBM Software) Grade 2 up (WIN CD)

Lamb Chop Loves Music CD (Phillips Media Software) Grades 1-3 (MAC/WIN CD)

Making Music CD (Voyager) Grade 2 up (MAC/WIN CD)

Microsoft Musical Instruments CD (Microsoft) Grade 4 up (MAC/WIN CD)

Opening Night CD (MECC) Grades 3-12 (MAC/WIN CD)

Thinkin' Things, Collections 1, 2, & 3 Grades PreK–8 Edmark (MAC/WIN CD)

Creative Movement: A Step Towards Intelligence (1993, Kultur)

Classic Composers Series (1987, Telemusic)

Kids Make Music (1994, Music Rhapsody)

Leonard Bernstein's Young People's Concerts (1990, Video Music)

Video Dictionary of Classical Ballet (1983, Kultur)